Peter & the Concrete Jungle

Peter & The Concrete Jungle ©2017 Maura Lee Bee. Published in the United States by Vegetarian Alcoholic Press. Not one part of this book may be reproduced without expressed written consent by the author. For more information, please contact *vegalpress@gmail.com*

ISBN-13: 978-0-9992103-7-6

Cover art by Samuel Prowse

TABLE OF CONTENTS

Introduction

Peach Cobbler//1
The Lost Boys//2
Finding Shelter//3
Blowfish//4
Yeshiva//5
Amourosity II//31
8:15//32
Isobel//33
When They'd Gone//34
Amourosity IV//35
Oma//36
Twelve Months Before HRT//38
Heart Surgery//39
When You Time Travel//40

Still Wonder//42

Mama's Cookies//47
Amourosity I//48
Home Economics//49
A Trip to the Met, 2008 - Living Photographs by Shigeyuki Kihara//50
Amourosity III//51
8:15, April 23rd//52
First Date//53
Bits of Glass//54
Grocery Shopping//55
Last Night//56
Tomorrow, Devotion//57
North Star//58

Afterward

Acknowledgements

To the lovers
the survivors
and the brightest of the
stars
xoxo

Introduction

I have this very vivid memory from when I was a child: there was a boy in my first-grade class who was telling everyone that he got a tap solo in his dance class. It was to a song in *Oliver!* and essentially, he was Oliver. Everyone started laughing at him, saying that "dancing is for girls."

And when I was six years-old, pigeon-toed in my denim dress, hiding behind the bangs my mother cut in the middle of our dining room, I stomped my foot and said passionately, "Tap-dancing boys are *cool*."

This is where it all began.

I was never a firm believer in the traditional gender role or just a binary view of gender. Some of my earliest memories include: my mother's combat boots; my mother, shaving her hair into a mohawk in our tiny, dim bathroom; my mother, obsessively buying convertible cargo pants for everyone in our family because they were practical and comfortable. We traded sneakers instead of makeup tips; she wore trousers and a blazer when someone sent her a passive aggressive email about "dress code" at work; and she would shave her head if it got to be over ninety-degrees. My mother was a gender warrior.

Despite the fact, however, that my mother grew up butch, and everyone expected her child to be the same, she sat through every tea party, drove me to countless dance classes, and bore through the pink-toys-and-cute-tiny-animal aisles because it brought me joy.

In a conversation with my editor, I told her about how my mother accepted me for who I was and never forced me to conform to society's ideals but to discover who I was on my own. "She is who she is," she would explain to her friends. And it was only after I became an adult that I realized not a lot of people were raised that way.

It was a surprise to everyone when I came out. I was so feminine, who could I be? I only wore pants when it got cold out, regularly watched makeup tutorials, and was constantly cast as the mother figure in community theater. Through many of my more formative years, I actually dealt with a lot of what we call gender issues, and was constantly asking myself about who I was and where I was going to be. There was no question about being a creative, a writer, a friend, but when it came to *seeing* myself, that was a much more difficult reality to face.

Over years of trial and error, I came to realize who I was, with some help along the way from many friends who have inspired this project. When I was thirteen, I knew I wasn't heterosexual; not six years later, in a room not much bigger than a closet, someone presented me with the articulation of myself: Queer. The fact was that I often found myself more attracted to people who were fluid in their expression, not to mention the fact that gender—in most ways—meant very little to me in terms of my expression.

So, I did research, and reading, and talked to everyone I knew. I met so many people with varying experiences and expressions, and it was only after a few months of focus on the subject of queerness that Peter came to be.

Peter came out of experience. He came out of the life stories people shared with me. He came out of the hardships which I heard and empathized, and Wendy came right along with him. I will not deny that both characters have aspects of people whom I know and care about very deeply, but at the end of the day, Peter and Wendy are very much their own beings. I did not expect this project to get to be the size that it is, however, after countless revisions and personal readings, I realized that there was *more*. That Peter and Wendy *wanted* to share their story with the rest of the world.

There is a great importance in this narrative. All too often, the transgender community gets pushed off to the side. In thirty-three states, a transgender person can still legally be fired from their job. Every day in the news, it is a constant battle for children's rights, bathroom rights, and general education for people within and outside of the LGBTQ+ community. Still, journalists insist on using the wrong gender pronoun. Still, people accept the theory that gender and sex are the same thing when they are not. Still, transgender people are victims of violent crime, discriminatory evictions, and are even killed in the name of belief. Still, it's an uphill battle, and every day there is another transgender person silenced due to hatred.

Which is why sharing stories is so important. I know that Peter's individual story is not mine to tell, which is why I present his section as more of a retelling. He is right at the brink of his journey, making new discoveries about himself and the world around him.

There is a great importance to the literary voice of a transgender character.

Peter's voice demands to be listened to and deeply felt.

I will admit outright that I don't know everything, but I am always willing to learn and listen to others. I will reiterate that I did not expect the project to be what it is today. At its core, this is the story of two people, of how they evolve, how they transition in life together.

When I was small, my parents never read me *Peter Pan*. I read my childhood copy to myself on the floor, as I did with many books. Perhaps it was always meant to be me with Peter and Wendy all along.

"When the first baby laughed for the first time, its laugh broke into a thousand pieces, and they all went skipping about, and that was the beginning of fairies."

Peter

Peach Cobbler

Peter didn't like
the peach cobbler
his mother taught him
how to make.
The lips of the dough,
were too sugary,
the space between
pink and warm
with the heart
of the fruit
and sticky with
preserves
when he
stuck his hands inside.
It was always
too sweet;
he much preferred
meals with
meat.

The Lost Boys

Peter fell asleep before he ran
Up through the trees, cuts on his hands
Blood like old jam never can
Come out from playing or understand

Up through the trees, cuts on his hands
from little thorns and acorn tails
Come out from playing, or understand—
He clawed the dirt out from his nails.

From little thorns, and acorn tails,
and squirrels that cackled through their scruff,
He clawed the dirt out from his nails:
The boys would always call his bluff.

And squirrels that cackled through their scruff
Haunted him until he wanted to die.
The boys would always call his bluff,
and he was not allowed to cry.

Haunted him until he wanted to die;
To Peter, death he could not fear.
And he was not allowed to cry:
They were always near.

To Peter, death he could not fear,
yet he was still aware
they were always near,
and what he hated was always there.

Yet he was still aware
when he ran footraces in cemeteries, six-years-young.
And what he hated was always there,
and he never dusted the mirror when he woke.

Finding Shelter

He built a house around him made of sticks and wood and a sheet from the hall closet and Mother told him   NO and he went to take one from the dryer And his brother said *Mom will kill you* and Peter said **Good, let her.** Because the thing about Peter is he was never afraid.
He built a house around him made of cardboard and wood from the garage And his father never blew it down , even though it shivered when Peter crawled out of it and said, **Look Dad, Look what I made.** And his father got down on one knee and told him, *Son, you can't fit your life into tiny boxes.*

Blowfish

I.
When Mom and Dad
sent his Husky away
to a Pennsylvania farm
a year after his
Twelfth birthday

II.
The puffy body of
forgotten sea creatures
being prodded with sticks
Beaten harder each time
he begged the boys to stop

III.
His body
Death Valley in his chest
pelvis sinking instead
of reaching out
when his hands touched
the glass

what they don't tell you about betrayal
is that it tastes like
grapefruit

Yeshiva

You have to get an education, she said.
Peter's mother, hovering like a moth,
pointed toward the ceiling.

She said, *you could learn a thing or two.*
She said, *We do it because we're proud.*

Proud of what, Peter was
unsure. He shuffled on the couch,
clutching himself.

His mouth tasted like copper;
there he was, sinking into a cushion,
staring at the fan above,
patterns of a greeting
he knew to believe in.

June 28th, 1969: A woman can't wear pants without being arrested, or raped by a cop. Butches and dykes and drag queens cling to the shadows of underground bars. A prohibition of denim and glitter. *Somewhere In St. Louis* flies off an immigrant's tongue. Blue suits came and raised a stir. Martha P. Johnson, the queen with flowers growing in her hair, shattered the glass ceiling, and together, they burned it down. It's too bad Judy Garland had died; she would have sung into the flames.

And her mother's mother went
And her mother
And then his mother
And then now it's you.
His brother still had his yarmulke,
buried in the sock drawer of his room.

A circle of white
with a burst of blue
At nine, Peter asked if that was his halo
and his mother told him to hush

His brother,
bringing two fingers to
each side of his head
began to hiss.

1973: Imagine a jumpsuit hugging a calf. Spanish in the back of her throat. Crowd rattling with displaced anger. Have you ever felt a man's angry fist? Imagine losing everything, including the clothes on your back. Imagine a crown soaked in the Hudson River. Open a hand, place in it your hopes and desires. Throw it into the screaming mob, pitchforks and all. This is what we call a sacrifice. Do you know what it's like to sleep in the rain, and still have something to fight for? *Y'all treat me like shit.* Sylvia is yelling, her curly hair a riot. *Y'all better quiet down.*

She said, *Don't you want God to love you?*

New Years Eve, 1993: A high school rite of passage. Point and tell the boy to drop his pants. When will the other boys and girls laugh with them? The joy ride towards misery, flying down the interstate. They take him and they
and   ,

Not listening. A rape kit will be torn fabrication, seams breaking. Like all horror shows, two boys with guns will pull him by the ankle out from under the bed. He will claw for his life.

Brandon Teena was killed in cold blood. His epitaph: erasure. Sometimes, we sit up, remember, and sob.

The rabbi is a nice man,
quiet man, still man,
Rocket man, manmade
sculpt of kosher leather
and thick frames.

He sees Peter,
awkward in loose jeans,
thick sweaters that
his mother bought
stretched by hand
away from the body,
dirty All Stars
covered in
ballpoint pen.

The rabbi is a nice man,
quiet man, still man,
a caring
man,
a fine
fellow

1998: *We know the story of Matthew Shepard, a college student in Laramie. But let me tell you the story again so you remember this time:*

Matthew was tied to a fence. Matthew was tied to a fence by two men he did not know. Matthew was tied to a fence by two men he did not know and beaten. Matthew was tied to a fence and beaten and kicked by strangers until he stopped moving. Matthew was tied to a fence and beaten and left there for eighteen hours. Matthew was tied to a fence, found supine—perfect Christ figure—succumbing to martyrdom in less than six days.

In Hebrew,
Matthew means
a gift

If Peter was a god-fearing man,
this would mean something to him.
If Peter was a Christian,
he would think that shepherds always walk back Home.

All Peter knows
is the translation
written in crooked script.

December 21st, 2001: Terrianne Summers, a 51 year-old trans woman and activist is shot in her front yard. The police did not consider it a hate crime, despite her hyper visibility. Her killer will likely never be found.

Peter can feel something
burning in his gut;
he isn't sure if he will throw up
or explode. Pale boy sits
on a velvet bench,
arms welded to himself,
the fabric pulling.
His shoulders and the zipper
are arguing, and Peter is sure
his body might win.

He thought this was about being closer to God,
and his mother turned to the salesperson
in contempt.

February 2008: Three trans women are abused and killed within ten days of each other. Duanna Johnson is beaten by police in a Tennessee detention center. Her body will be found months later, a collage of a person between bullet holes. Ashley Sweeney is shot in the head in Detroit. Sanesha Stewart is stabbed in the Bronx. It's not even one hundred days into the new year, and here they are, in the Bermuda Triangle of tragedy. A perfect storm.

Where do you see yourself in ten years?
Married. Maybe with a dog.
There is this hesitation
in his throat.
Is that right?
The rabbi poises himself,
a crane at the edge of a river flowing

Yes?
Peter turns to The Book of Esther
and wonders when he will
put on his mask
and start to save the world.

November 2008: Duanna's body is found. Lateisha Green is shot and killed in Syracuse. Her name, erased like her spirit from the earth, by arrogant journalists and fragile things. Her killer is brought to justice, and this is only the second time a person is convicted of transgender hate crime in The United States.

Now, crucifix falls into place. Make sure to bring pictures to the altar.

Peter, his mother said, *Don't you want to be a woman?*

March 30th, 2010: Amanda Gonzalez-Andujar is found dead in her Queens apartment. She was strangled and coated in bleach. Her defense attorney, at her killer's sentencing of twenty nine to life, asked the judge, "Shouldn't that sentence be reserved for people who are guilty of killing certain classes of individuals?"

Can you believe a human life is sacred?
Can you believe her family loved her?

One day with the rabbi:
I'm glad that Jews don't name us after the dead.
The older man's glasses
slid down his nose
with curiosity
Bad karma? he responds.
Peter shakes his head.
So we won't disappoint them.
The rabbi's head teeters
like a ball at the
edge of a roof.

Two months that start with A. Two friends, killed with love in their gums. Paige has a bullet through her cheek, and Tiffany was stabbed in the heart. Each killed for how they best showed their devotion: outside, inside. Don't forget to watch them run and play.

                                    Look at Peter,
                    scrolling through his holy book
                                listing the saints
                                       one by
                                       one by
                                         one.

2012: Jenna Talackova is running for Miss Canada. She wants to be the Queen of the Universe. Perhaps there's hope, when a leg can strut a stage, when a perfect bikini cut makes us human. Still, an article reminds us of a name long dead, and why the world is cold and cruel.

Why can't I wear a suit?
Peter asks both his mother
and the rabbi.

His mother
hands whirring
can't even answer.
She spits
and
tells him
not
to
bring
shame
or was it
pride
to the party.
He should be grateful
to have such an honor.

Rabbi laces
fingers together,
gestures his thumbs a spire.
Why can't you wear a suit?
he repeats, but Peter
already knows the answer.

December 28th, 2014: Leelah Alcorn leaps into oncoming traffic. Her dress a flutter, like the heart when it's finally satisfied, and she will be remembered as the final gift to the gods. Her death: a love song to semis. Her body: a public outcry. Her parents, in denial, will omit the name from a stone overgrown. The translation for Leelah is hard to find, but if one goes digging deep enough, it comes from the Sanskrit word for "play."

Look at Peter:
he is building a museum
for the martyrs:
photographs,
candles, and tape.

trying to stick them back together
trying to bring them back to life.

February 2016: Kayden Clarke suffers another meltdown, but this time his dog can't help him. Samson steps aside, like a good boy. The woman at animal rescue called the police. Check on him, like golden retrievers check on treasure. He is distressed. He is in danger of himself. The officers end the impending doom by bringing it to the present.

Kayden used to bring Christmas trees to those in need.

Where do the gifts go?

Peter is singing,
reciting his coming of age:
Dayenu, Dayenu, Dayenu
Dayenu, Dayenu...

Statistics are meaningless, if you can't remember all of their names. Monica Loera, 43. Jasmine Sierra, 53. Kayden Clarke, 24. Maya Young, 25. Demarkis Stansberry, 30. Kedarie/Kandicee Johnson, 16. Quartney Davia Dawsonn-Yochum, 32. Shante Thompson, 34. Keyonna Blakeney, 22. Reecey Walker, 32. Mercedes Successful, 32. Amos Beede, 38. Goddess Diamond, 20. Deeniquia Dodds, 22. Dee Whigham, 25. Skye Mockabee, 26. Erykah Tijerina, 36. Rae'Lynn Thomas, 28. T.T. Saffore, 28. Crystal Edmonds, 32.[1]

Keep in mind this is just the United States. Keep in mind that these names do not include those who have been injured, raped, maimed, and left for dead, but still survive. Keep in mind that this does not include those who still live in fear.

Read the list. Remember them.

---

[1] A list of transgender, gender non-conforming, and genderqueer people killed in 2016.

Peter's back to the wall,
watching the light skate through
temple windows.

Verse like a rap
stuck in God's teeth;
a golf clap
from all the mothers in the room.

The rabbi offers
a pat on the shoulder
a prayer shawl of his own
a card in folded paper.
He smiles, disappears among the
mozzerella sticks and
buffalo wings.

Peter opens the card
and inscribed inside is this:
Yasher koach
Today, you are a man.

His heart an engine,
combusting to start.
He hid the card in his coat pocket.
There was something,
of what he wasn't sure,
but this was
enough.

Amourosity II

He sat on the floor of the living room
eating pizza crust and dreaming
again of the days falling slowly
behind him, dripping as sweat does
on cold Sunday mornings

And between his mother's rom-coms,
and arguing with his brother over
who would get to use the tv next,
he would lay on the floor
and count the crooks in the ceiling
the way he would count stars

He would tap the air,
the outline of imaginary sparks
waiting for something,
something he could not understand
just yet.

He asked his brother how girls taste,
and he said it depended what lipgloss they're wearing,
and Peter couldn't help but wonder
for years
how he could love the flavor of someone else's lips
if he didn't even know how his own must taste

8:15

In the shadow of the concrete jungle,
in the warmth of the future unfolding

She held conversations
the way a surgeon holds a heart
just before the transplant,
even if there's only a
50/50 shot.

The day she moved next door,
her body draped over the window sill,
stars on her lips like feathers
clung to the air underneath,
he couldn't look away

He was sitting on the roof,
waving at the memories of cicadas,
emerald ivy draped over his sneakers.
Her voice carried,
pebbles against the pipes

And she called across the blanket
of April heat and pink. What are you
doing. He kicked his shoes
to the grass below, smiling like
she was smiling.
He said,

Flying.

Isobel

Her hair tasted of
overwhelming earth –
blueberries and cardamom
and her arms fanned
like wings did
when she wrapped her arms
around his
waist

Like Peter,
she believed
the world could end
if you looked at it
the wrong way.

Like Peter,
she could have sworn
she'd flown up rivers
unsinking as a body
of children on hot summer days

But when Peter was boyish,
she was sharp and unwilling
kicking at knotted trees
She never kissed the bee stings
or his mouth again

He would say he truly loved her,
but it would be true to say
that she made him stop believing,
and he never clapped again.

When They'd Gone

And each time they plucked
A smudge of color off him
He withered again

Never leave, he said
Reflection growing endless
Covering what bloomed

Sitting in the room
Ghosts and sadness in his mouth,
Peter's buds, clean split

Watered just by spit
Posture poor, growing question
Buried and rooted.

Amourosity IV

Before he knew what CPR felt like
Before he tasted cinnamon just before sleep
Before the fire in his bedroom cabinet
Before his mother cried and cried
Before the photographs gone
Before the murmurs of forever
Before freedom's true taste
Before his mother cried and cried
Before the birth of her son

After the first death, he said
After the smoke cleared away
After he stopped smelling like sadness
After the cloves were sprinkled
After the warmth of her soft face
After he stopped scrubbing it away
After forever
After forever
After forever
After Peter stopped growing
and became a child again.

Oma

The lounger smelt like elderberries,
and a nurse was burning wicks
soaked in rosewater and old lemon.

Her eyes were restless marbles
contained to a liquor store bag. Trapped,
her grey curls in spirals around her chin.

She looked at the child,
now a full foot taller. What was the term for it?
She chewed on a soft mint,
sugar gooing in her cheek.

She remembered her name,
Chaya. Daughter of Samuel,
wife of Paul, his memory a wisp.

Her eyes, searching for clarity.
Still, dense fog.
Still, a word out of reach.

And sometimes, he brought books with him—
not those holy books the nurses had—
but novels, comics, encyclopedias, to help her remember.

She tripped over Peter's name,
the rock of aphasia just under foot.
Tears ran from the length of his cheeks.

Her *grandson,*
sitting in the high back chair,
wrists folded across his lap,
copy of *Catcher in the Rye* on the floor.

The clouds moved across the blue,
and the light came pouring
through the water-stained window.

Peter held his Oma tight,
fingers trembling on her floral back:

two parentheses wrapped around a fondness.

This is the moment
Peter will never forget,
his grandmother stumbling
over her grandmother tongue,
English long forgotten.

Bracha,
he mouthed.
Tomorrow the blessings would come.

Twelve Months Before HRT

His chest was full of rocks,
and he could feel the gravel scratching his throat
the way bears scratch pine trees
to mark where they hunt.

But Peter stopped playing outside,
when he watched two boys get in a fist fight
with a truck behind the high school.
He got hit by a car once.
The mirror was his souvenir.

When it came to him,
Peter preferred to lay face up,
he'd at least
get to see what would crush him next.

He had been sick all morning,
because January had not treated them well.
He made soup like the kind his best friend's
mother made. Before the arthritis
broke her spirits as one breaks sticks for kindling.
It was the only way he ate vegetables.

The soup sat on the table,
closing in on itself.

My name is Peter,
and his voice echoed like
when he went camping with
his father.

I prefer to be called he.
He wrung his hands like a bathmat,
crumpling his expectations,
a paper bag
empty.

Heart Surgery

Doctor Abignale presses cold stethoscope to cold chest,
Breathe in breathe out, his Spanish accent wraps around his heart.

Peter taps his fingers in the waiting room, waiting for it to start,
It's beating so fast, it might give up, his heart.

No signs of problems, no unknown disease,
no cancer, no meds, minus what prevents a breaking heart.

We will lower your dose the first week following.
He understands, though there's a twinge in his heart.

He flips through pamphlets of scar tissue under bone,
a lotus opening over water, lightening his heart.

PLASTIC SURGEON, he reads over and over on the wall
and he loves this Doctor with all of his heart.

It will be just like falling asleep, while they pull him apart,
removing what's not his, giving him a new heart.

                    He could have sat him on his knee,
                        told him about
                        the girl who waited
                        who bought new band-aids
                    every night
                    so he'd always have
                    a different color;
                    the boy who never grew up
                    but learned to be.

            When the sun wraps itself up
        at the end of an August evening,
            his smile is crooked,
            and when Wendy asks about
    the journey of day into night,
he tells her about their adventure
until she falls asleep.

When You Time Travel

The lighthouse cast two shadows
reaching out to each shore line
to keep the north and south
within arms reach,
and a little boy points and asks him,
Mister, how did you get those scars?

He could tell him stories
of sharks, crocodiles, or
other mysterious creatures of
the blue;
He could say flying, an incident
with pirates or
mermaids;

Instead he says
Heart surgery.
It's automatic,
like the way he woke up
and put band-aids on his thumbs
to keep them from bleeding
after he spent all night
punching the picture frames
that remained in the mind
of the house where
he grew up

Still Wonder

For a moment the circle of light was broken   they felt rather lonely.   His sobs woke Wendy, and she sat up in bed,

even these noises ceased.   "I am the only one who is ~~not~~ afraid".
They were just everyday questions
he could not help looking solemn

She did not understand even now.   "Are you here?"
Peter was not quite like other boys.

He was afraid at last.   they had long lost count of the days,
it was not really Saturday night.

"What is it, Peter?"
she said.   His reluctance,
for almost the only time in his life.

Watching Peter with glistening eyes
Then he burst into tears, and the truth came out.
She had to take his hand.
Peter was such a small boy that one tends to wonder   about   the others
hatred of him

they are not really friendly to Peter.

He looked at her uncomfortably.
Neither of them understood the other's language.   there was breaking in his voice
                                        passing queer
                She did not understand even now.
Her mouth opens   They go on with their recollections
Her arms were extended toward Peter
She let her hands play in the hair of the tragic boy
                    Something in the righthand corner of her mouth
                                                                                "I remember kisses"

She could see nothing but what she thought was a shooting star.
            when brought near each other, would join like drops of water
                        She would wear his kiss on the chain around her neck
Wendy's heart went flutter
                                                            "I'll teach you to jump on the wind's back"
                                    He moaned
                                a sigh of relief,
                                a kind of adventure
                                    woke into life
                                    it was real now
                                                    he had one of his dreams that night
the first of many joyous evenings   she had believed in him
                                        the loveliest tinkle as of golden bells
                                        the breathing of little stars,
                                        straight on til morning.

"She dreamt that the Neverland had come too near and that a strange boy had broken through…"

Wendy

Mama's Cookies

The roll of dough
makes a mess on the table,
but Mama never minds
the mess.

I press an M&M thumb print
in each one with my hands
that would never be big enough
to hold a balanced grapefruit.

My dress is sticky with sugar
and the thin plastic packaging—
Years later, Mama would wonder
where my love of baking came from,

at what point I became
my idea of a woman,
when the recipe was never mine,
and why the kitchen was always
covered in flour and
polka dot aprons.

Amourosity I

I am cradling in oily palms
Scissors in one hand
My Mary Kay doll in
The other

At ten I give her marker highlights
of sleepless sunsets over
opening gold
And right then I snip them away

Synthetic hair glittering my toes
And legs shaven the first time
I grab her brunette opposite
And shove their faces together

Tearful, I stare at the scene and think
I'm too old to be playing anymore

Home Economics

Awkward students
rubbing flouring hands
snow that hasn't been baked
melting in the afternoon heat
It doesn't smell right,
Rachel says with chocolate on her nose,
there aren't berries in this

The boy who sits behind me
asks me for the second time
Why don't you think you're hot?
Because that's not what people say
I want to reply
but the oven just told us
to put the cake inside

The girl from the second group
winks at me as she licks her fingers clean
and as my classmate asks me a third time
I hear the conversation
across the table from me
about how some people
should just end their lives
because they would never
be angels anyway

I knock the back of their head
with a cook book,
and hit the wall
over and over and over
with their cheek bone
the teacher tells me to leave the room
The oven beeps endlessly
The cake is too dense,
Rachel admits to my shoulder

The cake crumbs behind me
under coating blue

A Trip to the Met, 2008 - Living Photographs by Shigeyuki Kihara

There is a little boy who
points at my best friend
and screams like cars on impact,
MOMMY IS THAT A BOY OR A GIRL

Rachel cut her hair,
donated it to cancer.
The mother says,
I don't know what IT is.

    There is a photo of a figure in Victorian skirts on a beach
        and under the caption there are no pronouns at all
           and I turn my head and look at them
            look at them until they fade into the
                images of topless folks, who
                  may be men or women
                    or both or noneatall
                      or the same
                        without
                        grins

I am smart enough to know
that a woman is a woman is a woman,
but I look at Rachel, then the mother, then the son,
and I think: what a monster.

Amourosity III

There is something about old lovers
that we see within ourselves,
eye colors close
the same CD collection
questions we've asked for years.

For a long time
I was attracted to people with glasses,
and I wonder if it had to do
with wanting to see
my reflection
in the other person
for the sentence
never to end
because the
loops of pictures
would be
unpunctuated

And then I realized that
too many men
too many women
too many people
didn't want to see themselves
staring back

I asked him once,
What am I?
He said quietly
I don't know

Love is a lot like
the end of a story,
but I have yet to experience it
except in a reflection—
for I was never me,
but rather a pixie
they made me out
to be.

8:15, April 23rd

I am having a panic attack,
diaphragm spazzing. Chest filling
with ghosts. Body twitching
like a tuning fork
like a vinyl string

In the shadow of the concrete jungle
in the warmth of the future unfolding

You grab my hand. Wipe away
tumbling balls of water. Flannel sleeves
like the underside of docks.
You catch the words before they
can trip over themselves.

And your face is so familiar.
Had I met you long ago,
hands smooth like stones
at the bottom of the ocean?
Was there stardust in your teeth
too?

First Date

His eyes
Puddling fire, gold
and fear
Clutching the stick shift
like a reluctant invitation
to the past

My hands
Opening in my lap
I want to hold all of his problems
on an invisible plate
and deliver them to someone else

The car smells like pizza
He tastes like oranges
and saltwater
when he leans over and kisses me

I won't be his giver
until the third date
And his cheek is pressed to my chest
I am too afraid
Of what I might leave behind

Bits of Glass

He fit together
as church windows do:
reds meeting
blues meeting
yellows and greens
meeting at a single
distorted scene

pictures like his childhood
bruised like day-old bananas
pictures like his mother's photographs
leaving the taste of dysphoria in his mouth

I haven't been to church in years
but when I met Peter
he was my baptism
he was a splash of water
in the still of the desert sun,
he called like gold binding
connecting and curling against
warped window panes
and confessions

please know you weren't my savior
the same way that I was the Bar Mitzvah
you never had.

Grocery Shopping

His hands corrode the wheel
with the sweat of ancient summers.
I can't tell if the slick water lines
are a river leading from his temples
or under his eyes.

We put away the oranges,
the bananas, the whole wheat bread.
I don't want to talk about it anymore,
and he wrings a dish rag
between his wrists and thumbs,

mourning a conversation
that's just at the corner of his mouth.
The cheese goes in the shelf,
that's where it always goes,
he says, *and where it always will be.*

He pulls out two slices,
kills the last of the rice milk,
tells me not to throw away the juice,
Not yet, and he pours me a glass
after examining the date again.

Garage sale plates clank
against the wooden table from his mother's.
I don't want to talk about it,
and I comply,
and he pats his chest twice
to feel it still   there.

Last Night

The mirror is dirty
with fingerprints,
the spot where I can trace
the scars
just above where you
breathe.

Clips of my garter
hold on to my stockings
like a child on a crowded street
stays with their mother.

I notice the little things.

The gap in my teeth
chipped blue nail polish
the crook of hair between
each covered leg,
the spot that I forgot to shave

your smile
over my shoulder
through the half-opened
door to your
living room slash
bedroom,
the smell of your cologne
I can taste the ocean
in my mouth tonight.

Tomorrow, Devotion

A cascade of light
through a high placed window;
peonies bursting
from oversized white vases;
a trail of red carpet,
and the other half
of a closed locket.

Funeral homes,
cold and uneasy.
Peter steps carefully
around a stuffed dog
in the hallway.
Owned by Sandy &
Lois Duncan,
says a plaque on the
white collar.

He stands at the back of the room,
arms a tremble, suit a bracket
in this defining verse.

One could say,
she truly loved her husband,
until the day they buried
his oldest shoes.

One could say,
she lived devoted to God,
until she forgot the wrinkled words
of dusty Talmuds.

One could say,
she was the kindest person they knew,
and Peter clutched himself,
hovering over a verse,
crying and crying
and crying.

North Star
~~A letter to Peter~~

I heard that when I was born,
Beanie Babies and Talkboys were the most
wanted presents in America
that holiday season:
So tell me why my entire life,
All I've ever wanted was the sweetness of love
not at the tip of my tongue,
but stuck to my outstretched fingers like frozen raspberries

How is it that by the age of ten,
I had eight baby dolls,
and by thirteen, between being home alone
or creative suffocation
I had eighteen nightmares about infertility
and eight hundred reasons to wait
until the Christmas story I wrote every year came true

I was wrapped up in paper and tape,
peeking through the slivers of red and green edges,
and with sweaty palms asking for something I could not have.
Why is it that love is like asking for a bike every year,
and getting gameboy after gameboy after book
and my parents wondering why
I'm always indoors,
pleading to open my mind when the ribbons are pulled too tightly,
darling, you were the only one with scissors sharp enough.

Your voice made my heart feel like it was
coated with tablespoons of cinnamon,
the flecks and sprinkles of each nutmeg mention
you ever made about how you'd never let me go.
I never told you this, but between family gatherings,
I used to wonder how you'd like the cranberries,
imagine how you'd laugh at every awful, Spanish joke,
only to ask me to translate later:
laughter then, that was secret, like every letter I left for Santa Claus
after I turned sixteen.

Your eyes were like gifts in advent calendars,
in them, I found something new every day, every moment,
but I still managed to find my way home
in every star that sparked and sculpted you
out of the atoms that once formed giant birds and tigers,
but lived in the minds of scientists and philosophers
because in a hundred thousand years with thousands of atoms,
I believe someone somewhere had to go, "We need to make him too."

You were a boy whose mind grew too fast for his body,
but I swear I'd garnish every word on your lips with a kiss
that would make mistletoe wilt and bloom twice as bright.
When I was a child, I once wrote a holiday story
and the teacher stopped and reread how I wrote "evergreen,"
but you were in every color, every green at the ends of tree branches
and lights that were out of my reach since infancy,
yet even now when I'm too short to reach them,
you are always willing to pull them down for me to touch

With you, I feel as warm as Chilean cocoa
on the iciest night in December,
and despite what you may think,
every moment was as magical as those
first drops of snow from the heavens,
like presents from God, waiting to be opened,
after the last white Christmas years before we touched.
Sometimes, I like to think our love was all I ever asked for,
but really, it was for you to bring me butterflies
even from the dust in the fireplace.

Acknowledgements

Thank you to the editors and staff of the following journals, blogs, and anthologies where many of my poems first appeared (in various forms): "Last Night," *Babbling of the Irrational* || "North Star," *Utopia Parkway*

Thank you to all of the people who read and inspired this book in its infancy. Nicole Cooley, Richard Schotter, Jo, Michael, Nat, Jordan and countless others. Thank you staff of TEDxCUNY for allowing me the opportunity to present my poems. Jake, Safanah, Cheyn, Simona, Meira, Linda, Eloise, thanks for listening and believing in Peter. Lisa Bernard, thank you for your patience and kindness. Thanks John Weir, for all the work you do and your constant inspiration.

Thank you Nathan Fredrick at Vegetarian Alcoholic Press, who was Team Maura when I needed it most. Thank you Sam Prowse for loving this project enough to make the beautiful cover art that graces this book.

Thank you to my loved ones. Emily, I will always be grateful for you. Thanks Mom for never teaching me to conform to gender roles, and being fabulous doing it! Thanks Nandi for always fighting for me. Thanks Dad for having no fear.

Thank you to my loving partner, who is endlessly supportive, even when it's not easy.

Finally, thanks to the people who are the stars in Peter's universe. Never stop believing. Never stop soaring. Never stop being true.

Queer lovers, this one's for you.

Notes

The opening quotes to Peter and Wendy's sections respectively are from JM Barrie's novel *Peter Pan* (1911).

Yeshiva: a school for talmudic study; an Orthodox Jewish rabbinical seminary; a Jewish day school providing secular and religious instruction.

The historical events and deaths, as well as translations, included in the poem, "Yeshiva" are as follows:

June 28th, 1969: The Stonewall Riots, in which a police raid occurred at The Stonewall Inn, a bar for "butch dykes and drag queens". Sylvia Rivera, Marsha P. Johnson and others were fed up with the brutality against their community, they started to throw anything from beer cans to parking meters at the cops. The officers hid in the bar, and the protestors set it on fire. The next day, they gathered, calling for liberation. Although this was not the end of police brutality—particularly against trans women of color—this event was pivotal and considered the beginning of Gay Liberation (Leitsch, Dick. "Acting Up at the Stonewall Riots." *Long Road to Freedom: The Advocate History of the Gay and Lesbian Movement.* Thompson, Mark., ed. Los Angeles: The Advocate, 1994. 28-29. Print.)

1973: Johnson and Rivera are banned from participating in the third annual Pride Parade, under the guise that they "weren't gonna allow drag queens". Their solution? To march at the front of the parade. At the Christopher Street Rally that same year, Rivera gave her iconic speech "Y'all Better Quiet Down." Twenty years later, Marsha P. Johnson's body is found in at the West Village Piers (Kasino, Michael "Pay It No Mind - The Life and Times of Marsha P. Johnson" (2012); "Y'all Better Quiet Down," Internet Archive).

New Year's Eve, 1993: Brandon Teena, an American trans man, is raped and killed in Humboldt, Nebraska, as well as Lisa Lambert, who owned the house he was living in, and Phillip Devine, a friend. Teena was outed, and received a rape kit, but it was never found. They were killed by John Lotter and Tom Nissen. Lana Tisdel, as well as her sister and mother, were heavily involved in criminal trials and lawsuits that followed the murder. Teena was 21 at the time of his death (*The Brandon Teena Story,* Dir. Susan Muska and Gréta Olafsdóttir, 1998). Teena's story was used as a way to lobby against hate crime.

1998: Matthew Shepard is killed in Laramie, Wyoming on October 6th. He was 22. The three suspects—Russell Henderson, Aaron McKinney, and Chastity Pasley—were all sentenced (Casper-Star Tribune archives). His story, like Teena's, was used as a way to lobby against transgender hate crime, in a law later signed called "The Matthew Shepard Act."

December 2001: Terrianne Summers is killed. She was 51 (Jaworski, Alexa. "LAW & DISORDER: Transgender activist found shot to death at Westside home." Florida Times-Union, Dec 14 2001).

February 2008: A video of Duanna Johnson being beaten by two police officers sparks attention of gay rights groups in February. The cops were condemned. In November, her body is found in downtown Memphis. She was 43 (Brown, New York Times). Ashley Sweeney, age unknown, is killed in Detroit. Sanesha Stewart is killed in the Bronx at 25 (Memorializing 2008, Transgender Day of Remembrance website).

November 2008: Duanna's body is found. Lateisha Green is shot in Syracuse, New York. She was 22 (Memorializing 2008, Transgender Day of Remembrance website).

March 30th, 2010: Amanda Gonzalez-Andujar is found dead in her Queens apartment. She was strangled. She was 29. Queens Supreme Court Justice Richard Buchter did not take too kindly to her defense lawyer not agreeing with his decision. "This court believes every human life in sacred," he said. "It's not easy living as a transgender, and I commend the family for supporting her." (Fishbein, Rebecca. "Lawyer:

Murdering A Transgender Prostitute Not Such A Big Deal." Gothamist, Dec 6 2013).

Two months that start with A: Paige Clay is shot and killed in Chicago in April 2012. She was 23. Three blocks away, in an unoccupied building, Tiffany Gooden is killed in August 2012. She was 19 (Memorializing 2012, Transgender Day of Remembrance website).

2012: Jenna Talackova runs for Miss Universe Canada, but is told she can't compete because she is transgender. She successfully waged a legal battle in order to compete (White, Nancy. "Jenna Talackova, transgendered Miss Universe Canada contestant, shines in spotlight." Toronto Star, May 18 2012)

December 28th, 2014: Leelah Alcorn posts her suicide note on her Tumblr after being forced into conversion therapy by her parents. She walks onto the interstate. She was 17. Her death, similar to Shepard and Teena, is used as an example of why conversion therapy should be illegal (an act named "Leelah's Law," which has yet to be passed) (Fox, Fallon. "Leelah Alcorn's Suicide: Conversion Therapy Is Child Abuse." Time, Jan 8 2015).

February 2016: A year earlier, a video of Kayden Clarke goes viral where his service dog Samson helps diffuse a melt down, where Clarke had the tendency to hurt himself. When performing a wellness check, Clarke had a twelve-inch knife in his hand, and despite having stun guns, the police killed him. He was 24 (Abeni, Cleis. "Arizona Trans Man Shot and Killed By Police in His Own Home." Advocate, Feb 6 2016).

Dayenu: A passover sedar song. In Hebrew, roughly translates to "it would have been enough."

Statistics are meaningless: A list of transgender, gender non-conforming, and genderqueer people killed (and how old they were) in 2016 in the United States.

Yasher koach: Hebrew for "good job," usually given to someone who has given a torah blessing.

Bracha: Hebrew for "blessing."

Still Wonder is a cento, compiled from JM Barrie's novel *Peter Pan* (1911).

A Trip to the Met, 2008 - Living Photographs by Shigeyuki Kihara: an ekphrastic poem inspired by the work of the same title, "Living Photographs" by Shigeyuki Kihara.

"Grocery Shopping" was inspired by Marie Howe's "The Gate."

www.ingramcontent.com/pod-product-compliance
Lightning Source LLC
Chambersburg PA
CBHW030457010526
44118CB00011B/975